Seeing the Mountain

How Zen made me a better Catholic

by Thomas C. Daniels

Seeing the Mountain
How Zen made me a better Catholic
Copyright © 2026 by Thomas C. Daniels. All rights reserved.

First Edition: June 2026
Published by One Dharma Zen, Tyler, Texas,
www.onedharmazen.org

CREDITS & ACKNOWLEDGMENTS
Cover and Interior Illustrations
Image credit: Mountain illustration created with Microsoft Copilot, based on prompts and direction by Thomas C. Daniels.
Translations: English translation of the Heart Sutra adapted from traditional Mahayana liturgical texts, as translated by Google Gemini. English translation of Noche Oscura del Alma (Dark Night of the Soul) adapted from the original 16th-century Spanish text of St. John of the Cross, as translated by Google Gemini.

Library of Congress Cataloging-in-Publication Data
Daniels, Thomas C.
Seeing the Mountain: How Zen made me a better Catholic / Thomas C. Daniels.
Library of Congress Control Number: 2026914156
ISBN: 9798996325122 (paperback)
ISBN: 9798996325139 (Kindle)
Printed in the United States of America

Dedication

To my son, Maison —
I have walked many paths to find the Mountain.
May your journey be gentler than mine,
your steps lighter,
and your heart always open
to the grace that waits for you.

Table of Contents

INTRODUCTION 2

The Threshold 2

Thomas Merton: The Bridge 2

The Mountain as Teacher 3

The Dark Night of Emptiness 4

Into the Dark Night of Emptiness: Juan meets Quan(yin)   4

Why I Wrote This Book 5

CHAPTER ONE 7

A Circle of Teachers 7

St. Thomas Aquinas 7

St. John of the Cross 7

Rabbi Moses Maimonides (RAMBAM) 7

Thích Nhất Hạnh 8

Zen Master Seung Sahn 8

Chinul (Bojo Jinul) 8

Jean-Pierre de Caussade 8

Thomas Merton 8

Mazu Daoyi 9

Myodo Jabo 9

The Presences 9

Avalokiteshvara (Quan Yin) 9

The Blessed Virgin Mary 10

Why These Guides Matter 10

CHAPTER TWO 13

St. Thomas Aquinas: The Simplicity of God 13

CHAPTER THREE 15

St. John of the Cross: The Dark Night as Doorway 15

CHAPTER FOUR 18

Rabbi Moses Maimonides (RAMBAM): The God Beyond
All Attributes 18

CHAPTER FIVE......21

Thích Nhất Hạnh: Interbeing and the Permission to Go
Home 21

The Pilgrimage to Huế 22

CHAPTER SIX......24

Zen Master Seung Sahn: The Flawed Buddha Who
Opened the Gate 24

CHAPTER SEVEN 27

Bojo Jinul (Chinul): Sudden Awakening, Gradual
Cultivation 27

CHAPTER EIGHT......30

Jean-Pierre de Caussade: The Jesuit Who Showed Me That
Zen Had Led Me Home 30

CHAPTER NINE 33

Thomas Merton: The Trappist Who Showed Me the
Bridge Was Always There 33

CHAPTER TEN 36

Mazu Daoyi: The Thunderous Ancestor Who Twisted My
Nose Awake 36

CHAPTER ELEVEN 40

The Permission Givers 40

Myodo Jabo — The First Permission: *"Your intentions are
pure."* 40

Thích Nhất Hạnh — The Second Permission: *"You can
go home."* 42

Thomas Merton — The Third Permission: *"You are not
alone on this path."* 43

Three Permissions, One Path 44

CHAPTER TWELVE.. 44

    The Mountain.. 44

    Silence and Simplicity.................................... 45

    The Sudden and the Slow............................ 46

    Twin Guardians of Mercy............................. 47

    How to Walk... 48

CHAPTER THIRTEEN... 49

    The Names We Are Given............................ 49

    The First Path: Thomas................................ 50

    The Radiant Seed: Quang Phúc Lạc............ 50

    The Iron Spine: Min'ui Maitri...................... 51

    Mandalas of the Heart................................. 52

CHAPTER FOURTEEN 54

    The Insight of St. John of the Cross: The Practice Manual
.... 54

        Noche Oscura del Alma 56

CHAPTER FIFTEEN.. 63

    The Perfection of Wisdom Heart Sutra: The Practice
Manual 63

CHAPTER SIXTEEN 71

    Juan Meets Quan(yin): The Moment of Recognition . 71

CHAPTER SEVENTEEN... 75

    Two Become One 75

EPILOGUE... 79

    The Mountain and the Mirror 79

AUTHOR'S NOTE 82

INTRODUCTION

The Threshold

There is a Korean Seon teaching that has followed me for years, like a lantern carried just ahead of my steps:

You can see Mount Jogye from the North as well as from the South.

I no longer remember where I first heard it. I only know that it became the compass of my spiritual life, a quiet reassurance when the terrain beneath my feet felt entirely divided. For me, the Mountain is God — the vast, silent, generative presence at the heart of all things. Zen taught me how to see the Mountain; Catholicism taught me how to meet the One who waits there.

This book is the story of how those two paths, which began on opposite sides of the world, converged in the landscape of my own heart.

Thomas Merton: The Bridge

Before I go any further, I need to introduce the Catholic priest who made it possible for me to fully appreciate Zen through the lens of a Catholic: Thomas Merton.

Long before I ever sat on a cushion, Merton had already walked into dialogue with Zen masters, corresponded with D.T. Suzuki, and recognized that the contemplative heart is universal. He never abandoned his Catholic faith; he deepened it by learning how other traditions approached silence, stillness, and the unspoken Word.

Merton once wrote that the analytical mind wants to look *at* things, but contemplation and Zen teach us to look *from* things — from a place of interior stillness where the ego no longer distorts what it sees.

When I discovered *Lectio Divina*, I realized that its final movement — *Contemplatio* — was nearly identical to the objectless, wordless awareness I had already encountered in Zen. Both practices move through the same progression:

— Beyond intellect

— Beyond concepts

— Beyond self

— Into silence

Merton gave me permission to trust that resonance. He is the doorway through which many Catholic readers will enter this book, and the doorway through which I first entered the contemplative life.

The Mountain as Teacher

One of my favorite authors writes that mountains are the great Ch'an teachers — vast, silent, generative, mirrors of the cosmos. Ch'an monasteries were built in mountains not for isolation, but because mountains embody the very qualities meditation seeks to cultivate:

— dramatic distances

— mirror-deep clarity

— silence that resounds

— presence without commentary

Meditation empties the mind of words and concepts, and the mountain reinforces that emptiness with its own vastness. The landscape itself becomes a teacher.

For me, the Mountain became a metaphor for God — not a distant deity, but a presence that is immense, quiet, and utterly simple. Zen cleared the vision so I could face that vastness without flinching;

Catholicism gave me the language of intimacy to speak to the
Presence waiting within it.

The Dark Night of Emptiness

Somewhere along the way, the teachings of St. John of the Cross
and the Heart Sutra began to echo each other in my mind. *Nada,
nada, nada* began to sound like *form is emptiness, emptiness is form*. The
dark night began to resemble the luminous void of Zen.

This convergence eventually found its way into a poem that became
the inner doorway of this book:

Into the Dark Night of Emptiness: Juan meets Quan(yin)

(Excerpt)

To arrive at what you do not know,

walk the path that unravels knowing.

To hold what you do not own,

let even the breath in your throat fall away.

Nada, nada, nada.

The sky collapses into the mirror,

the mirror shatters into light.

Form is emptiness, emptiness is form —

a landscape unwritten,

a silence that sees without eyes.

[...]

4

There is no path, no mountain, no prize —

only the luminous dark,

perfectly empty, perfectly awake.

This poem is not an argument. It is a testimony — the place where Juan de la Cruz meets Avalokiteshvara, where the dark night meets the Heart Sutra, where Catholic contemplation meets Zen emptiness.

It is the inner truth of this book.

Why I Wrote This Book

Zen has not replaced my Catholicism. Catholicism has not replaced my Zen.

Zen provides the emptiness; Catholicism provides the Mirror. Together, they teach me how to listen to the unspoken Word.

This book is my attempt to share that journey — to show how two ancient traditions, seen from opposite sides of the Mountain, reveal the same luminous simplicity at the heart of all things.

"Be still, and see that I am God."
Psalm 44:11 (Douay–Rheims)

CHAPTER ONE

A Circle of Teachers

Before I can tell you how Zen makes me a better Catholic, I need to introduce the companions who have walked with me — a circle of teachers whose voices come from different centuries, cultures, and traditions, yet somehow speak to the same interior landscape.

They are not arranged in hierarchy. They are not arranged by doctrine. They are arranged the way stars arrange themselves in the night sky — each shining with its own light, each helping me find my way.

St. Thomas Aquinas

The Architect of Christian Reason

He taught me that faith is not the enemy of clarity, and that the mind, when purified, becomes a form of prayer. He was the philosopher who ultimately became a mystic.

St. John of the Cross

The Poet of the Dark Night

He showed me that God is found not by accumulation but by subtraction — *nada, nada, nada* — a refrain that echoes the heart of the *Heart Sutra* more than many Catholics realize.

Rabbi Moses Maimonides (RAMBAM)

The Master of Apophatic Theology

He taught me that the closer we come to the Divine, the fewer words we can honestly use. His dynamic silence is the close cousin of Zen's emptiness, reminding us that the Divine is always encountered before thought.

Thích Nhất Hạnh

The Gentle Revolutionary of Mindfulness

He taught me *interbeing* — the radical insight that nothing exists alone, not even the self. His profound compassion softened my theology, opened my heart, and gave me the ultimate permission to "go home" to my Christian roots.

Zen Master Seung Sahn

The Thunderclap of Direct Seeing

The Korean monk with the sharp stick and the warm laugh. He taught me that truth is not an intellectual concept but an immediate, direct seeing, and that the mountain looks different from every side while remaining one mountain.

Chinul (Bojo Jinul)

The Synthesizer of Seon

The great master of the Korean tradition who mapped the rhythm of sudden awakening and gradual cultivation — a spiritual choreography that mirrors the Christian life far more than most Christians suspect.

Jean-Pierre de Caussade

The Apostle of the Present Moment

He taught me that God is found in the sacrament of the ordinary, inside the quiet "duty of the present moment". In his Jesuit cassock, he taught me the Catholic version of "Chop wood. Carry water".

Thomas Merton

The Bridge-Builder

He taught me that the contemplative heart is universal, showing that a Trappist monk in Kentucky can recognize a Zen monk in Kyoto as an intimate brother. He proved that Zen and Christian contemplation are simply two ways of entering the exact same silence.

Mazu Daoyi

The Thunderous Ancestor

The ancient Chan master whose words shock the mind awake. He taught me that awakening is never an elusive thing found elsewhere — "Mind is Buddha" — a teaching that startled me into recognizing the absolute nearness of grace.

Myodo Jabo

The Living Guide

My living Zen teacher, who taught me that sincerity matters far more than formal lineage, and that the Mountain can be approached from any side as long as the heart is true. When my practice felt fragmented, her immense clarity helped me trust my own unfolding, acting as a steady, quiet influence in my realization of non-duality.

The Presences

There are other companions on this path who are not teachers in the usual sense, but timeless presences of the heart:

Avalokiteshvara (Quan Yin)

The Bodhisattva of Compassion

Known in the West and across Asia by many names, including her Chinese incarnation as Quan Yin, she is the one whose thousand arms reach into every distinct corner of human suffering. In the silence of Zen, Avalokiteshvara sits and teaches me how to truly listen.

The Blessed Virgin Mary

The Mother of God

With a quiet, world-changing *fiat*, she opened the fabric of creation to receive the unspoken Word. In the heart of Catholicism, Mary teaches me how to receive.

These two stand on either side of my path like twin guardians of mercy. They are not characters in my story; they are the very atmosphere of it.

Why These Guides Matter

Some readers will know Aquinas but not Mazu. Some will know Thích Nhất Hạnh but not de Caussade. Some will know Mary but not Avalokiteshvara. Some will know Merton but not Chinul. Some will know Zen but not Catholicism — and some the reverse.

But every single one of them is pointing toward the same Mountain, the same silence, and the same luminous simplicity of God.

This is the company that has shaped me; this is the chorus that has taught me how to listen. This is the circle that makes it possible for me to say, without an ounce of contradiction:

— Zen has not replaced my Catholicism.

— Catholicism has not replaced my Zen.

They illuminate each other. They deepen each other. They allow me to be fully present.

"[O]ne thing is necessary."
Luke 10:42 (Douay–Rheims)

CHAPTER TWO

St. Thomas Aquinas: The Simplicity of God

I first met Thomas Aquinas not as a medieval philosopher, but as a quiet presence in the background of my early Catholic formation — a name spoken with reverence, a mind too large to ignore. Only later did I discover the man behind the legend : born in 1225 in Roccasecca, Italy, and raised in a noble family who fully expected him to become a powerful Benedictine abbot. Instead, he shocked them by joining the Dominicans — a ragtag band of mendicant preachers who embraced radical poverty and study.

His family was so outraged by this choice that they kidnapped him, locked him away in a fortress tower, and spent over a year trying to break his vocation. But Aquinas simply prayed, studied, and waited. When they finally released him, he walked straight back to the Dominicans. His calling was unmistakable.

He went on to study under Albert the Great in Paris and Cologne, absorbing Aristotle, Augustine, Scripture, and the entire intellectual architecture of his time. His classmates initially mocked him as "the Dumb Ox" because he was heavy-set, quiet, and slow to speak. Albert, however, famously silenced them, replying: "His bellowing will be heard throughout the world."

And he was right. Yet, what mattered most to me as I looked back on his life was not Aquinas's unmatched intellectual brilliance — though he was brilliant — but his profound humility before mystery.

In his masterpiece, the *Summa Theologiae*, Aquinas insists on a radical truth: God is not complicated. We are complicated; God is simple. He did not mean simple as in easy, but simple as in indivisible, unfragmented, and pure. God is not a being among other beings. God is *Being itself* — Pure Act, Pure Presence, Pure Simplicity. The closer we come to this reality, the less we can say — not because God is vague, but because the Divine is too intensely real for our fragile human categories.

This was my first genuine encounter with apophatic theology, long before I ever knew the word. Aquinas taught me that the intellect is a ladder — one you climb with absolute devotion and rigor — but a ladder you must eventually let go of.

And Aquinas himself let go of it.

Near the end of his life, after experiencing a profound mystical vision during Mass, he stopped writing altogether. When his secretary begged him to return to work and finish the *Summa*, Aquinas simply shook his head and said:

"All I have written seems like straw compared to what has been revealed to me."

That moment changed me. It was the exact moment Aquinas became, in my mind, a Zen monk without ever knowing it. He had reached the Mountain's summit. He had gazed directly into the absolute simplicity of God, and he knew that human words could go no further.

Zen had given me a raft; Aquinas gave me a ladder. Zen had taught me when to step off the raft, but Aquinas had already shown me that he knew how to set down the ladder, as well.

Most importantly, across centuries and traditions, he was the very first to whisper to me in the quiet of my own seeking: *God is simpler than you think.*

CHAPTER THREE

St. John of the Cross: The Dark Night as Doorway

By the time I truly encountered St. John of the Cross, I was already deep into Zen practice. I had taken vows, received Dharma names, and lived for years inside the deep silence and discipline of Buddhist meditation. Because of this, I thought I understood emptiness; I thought I understood unknowing. I even believed I had already walked through the dark night of the soul through my own battles with PTSD, depression, and fatalism.

Then I met Juan de la Cruz.

John was born Juan de Yepes y Álvarez in 1542 in the rugged, sun-bleached plains of Castile, Spain. His childhood was defined by severe poverty and profound loss; his father died young, and his mother struggled desperately just to keep the family alive. Hardship shaped him early, but so did a quiet, inherently contemplative temperament. Even as a young boy, he found himself drawn inexorably to prayer, to silence, and to the hidden life of the soul.

He entered the Carmelite Order in his early twenties, longing for a life of radical simplicity and contemplation. But God had other plans. When he met Teresa of Ávila — fiery, brilliant, and utterly uncompromising — she immediately recognized in him a fellow traveler. She saw someone who replication-longed to restore the Carmelites to their original, unadulterated contemplative fire. Together, they began the Discalced Carmelite reform, a rigorous return to poverty, silence, and prayer.

It was a beautiful vision, but it was also incredibly dangerous. Institutional opposition grew, political tensions flared, and eventually, John was kidnapped by his own religious brothers. They imprisoned him in a tiny, suffocating cell, where he was regularly beaten, starved, and left entirely in the dark.

It was in that literal and spiritual darkness that he composed the fragments of poetry that would become *The Dark Night of the Soul*. Yet, the darkness could not contain him. After nine grueling months in that cell, John made a daring escape, crawling through a small window and fleeing into the safety of the night. The nuns of a nearby monastery took him in, tenderly nursed him back to life, and gave him the space to write the monumental commentaries that would shape Christian mysticism for centuries.

When I first read John's field reports from that darkness, I was stunned. Here was a sixteenth-century Christian mystic describing, with uncanny, clinical precision, the exact internal terrain I had been navigating on the meditation cushion through Zen:

— the stripping away of the separate self

— the systematic collapse of rigid concepts

— the silence that is not an empty void, but a luminous fullness

— the radical surrender of all mental images of God

— the profound unknowing that is infinitely deeper than human knowledge

His relentless refrain — *nada, nada, nada* — sounded like the *Heart Sutra* whispered in Spanish.

I had spent years practicing Zen before I ever opened John's writings, and yet when I did, I felt as if I were reading a familiar map drawn in a different script. Zen had prepared me for him. Zen had given me the tools to comprehend his depth, and it had taught me how to sit still enough to actually hear what he was saying.

Through him, I realized that the psychological torment of my trauma was not the same as the spiritual shedding of the mystic. John taught me that the true dark night is not God's agonizing absence. It is God's overwhelming presence in a form the ego simply cannot recognize. He showed me that the soul reaches the Divine not by accumulation, but by subtraction; not by grasping, but by letting go; not by seeing, but by the pure surrender of being seen.

And he taught me something else that resonated deeply with the very core of my Eastern training: the dark night is never the end. It is the beginning.

John of the Cross arrived late in my journey, but when he arrived, he spoke with absolute authority. He showed me that the path I had walked in Zen was never foreign to Christianity; it was already there, hidden deep within our own mystical tradition, quietly waiting for me to rediscover it. He taught me how to walk through the darkness without an ounce of fear, how to trust the absolute silence, and how to see that emptiness and God's hiddenness are not opposites at all.

When I imagine the Mountain now, I see John standing directly beside the Seon master Chinul. I hear both the Carmelite and the monk saying the exact same thing in two different tongues: *"Awakening is sudden. Transformation is gradual."*

More than any other Christian mystic, John prepared me for the final synthesis of my own unfolding — the sacred threshold where Juan meets Quan(yin) at the summit of the Mountain.

CHAPTER FOUR

Rabbi Moses Maimonides (RAMBAM): The God Beyond All Attributes

I encountered RAMBAM before I ever opened the *Summa Theologiae*, before I knew the language of Christian mysticism, and before I had any inkling that the apophatic path even existed in my own Western tradition. In many ways, RAMBAM was the first great voice who taught me that God is not something we grasp — God is something we release into.

Moses ben Maimon was born in 1138 in Córdoba, Spain, into the golden age of Andalusian Judaism — a brilliant world where philosophy, science, and faith lived in vibrant conversation. His early life, however, was marked by severe upheaval; religious persecution forced his family to flee across Spain and North Africa before finally settling in Egypt. There, he became a physician, a towering legal scholar, a community leader, and eventually the greatest Jewish philosopher of the medieval world.

He lived a grueling life of absolute service — tending to the sick by day, writing by night, and guiding his exiled people with a mind that never stopped seeking clarity. His vocation was not monastic, but it was deeply contemplative. He was a man who lived fully in the world while thinking entirely beyond it.

His masterpiece, *The Guide for the Perplexed*, was written specifically for seekers — for those who loved God deeply but struggled with the limits of language, the weight of tradition, and the agonizing complexity of the world. And in that book, RAMBAM makes a claim so radical that it entirely reoriented my understanding of the Divine:

We cannot say what God is. We can only say what God is not.

This was my first real encounter with true apophatic theology. This was my first genuine glimpse of the Mountain.

RAMBAM taught me that every positive attribute we assign to God — powerful, wise, loving — is ultimately a human projection, a limitation, and a distortion. God is not "a being" who possesses a collection of grand qualities. God is beyond all qualities.

Beyond all categories.

Beyond all conceptual grasp.

Relying on the ancient Hebrew of the Psalms, he wrote:

"Silence is praise to You."

When I first read that line, something deep within me shifted. It felt like the *Heart Sutra* whispered in Hebrew. It felt like *zazen* before I ever knew the word *zazen*. It was the first profound crack in the rigid shell of my inherited, childhood images of God.

RAMBAM taught me that the closer we come to the Divine, the fewer words we can honestly use. He showed me that silence is not the mere absence of speech — it is the very presence of truth. And he taught me something else, an insight that would shape the entire remainder of my journey: God's simplicity is not a philosophical abstraction. It is a rigorous spiritual practice.

To approach God, I had to let go of my images of God. To know God, I had to unknow God. To love God, I had to release the frantic self that tried so desperately to grasp Him. RAMBAM was the first teacher who showed me that the path to the Divine is a path of radical subtraction.

He was also the one who led me to Aquinas. Not the other way around.

When I later discovered that Thomas Aquinas had read RAMBAM, argued with his texts, absorbed his insights, and built his own theology upon his foundation, I felt a profound sense of continuity — as if I were following a hidden trail laid down centuries before I was born. Zen was the first step on that trail. RAMBAM was the next. Aquinas would come later, but the seed was already planted.

Years later, when I immersed myself in the study of Jewish mysticism, RAMBAM became one of my foundational guides. But he was not alone. Elie Wiesel's *Souls on Fire* introduced me to the Hasidic rebbes — men who argued with God, wept with God, and wrestled with the Divine. They taught me that God is not fragile, that relationship is not polite, and that the Mountain must be climbed with your whole, raw heart, not just your dynamic serenity.

RAMBAM gave me the silence; the rebbes gave me the fire.

Together, they taught me that God is simultaneously beyond all human attributes and intimately, beautifully present in the broken cries of the heart.

RAMBAM stands on the Mountain directly beside Aquinas, both of them pointing toward the exact same luminous simplicity. And he stands right beside the ancient Zen masters, who boldly declare:

"No eye, no ear, no mind."

He taught me that the God I sought was never elsewhere. Not hidden behind rigid doctrine. Not confined to exclusive tradition. He is present in the very act of letting go.

RAMBAM helped me see that the Mountain is not climbed by accumulating more beliefs, but by systematically releasing the ones that obscure the view.

Silence is not emptiness. Silence is God.

CHAPTER FIVE

Thích Nhất Hạnh: Interbeing and the Permission to Go Home

By the time I encountered Thích Nhất Hạnh, I had already been practicing Zen for a few years. I had immersed myself in Korean Seon, received Dharma names, taken formal vows, and begun walking the Bodhisattva path with deep sincerity. But when I found Thầy — or perhaps when Thầy found me — something fundamental in my practice shifted entirely from the head to the heart.

Thích Nhất Hạnh was born in 1926 in central Vietnam, ordained as a young novice at the age of sixteen at Từ Hiếu Temple in Huế — the very sanctuary where he would return, decades later, to spend his final earthly days. His long life was dramatically marked by war, exile, tireless peace activism, poetry, and a gentleness so profound that it felt like a living form of enlightenment itself. He was a monk, a teacher, a refugee advocate, a poet, and — to me — the closest thing to a living Buddha I have ever encountered.

I have read more of his books than any other author except the Holy Bible. His words have been intimate companions to me in ways I can scarcely describe. His signature teachings on *interbeing* — the radical insight that absolutely nothing exists alone, that everything is endlessly woven into everything else — completely reshaped the way I saw reality. Thầy taught me that God's presence is never confined to a distant heaven, a temple, or a church building, but is the very dynamic fabric of existence itself.

Yet, it wasn't just his sweeping philosophy that touched me. It was his sheer, radiant humanity.

His monumental poem *"Please Call Me By My True Names"* — especially the agonizing line about being simultaneously the sea pirate and the young refugee girl — broke something wide open inside me. It revealed a compassion so radical and all-embracing that it felt exactly like the Gospel spoken in a completely new tongue.

His simple Dharma talks on the art of flower arranging taught me more about authentic mindfulness than any dense, formal academic treatise ever could. His deliberate way of walking, breathing, and smiling — these were not merely instructions; they were teachings in themselves.

When I lived in Houston, I regularly sat retreats with the monks and nuns he had ordained into the Order of Interbeing. Their physical presence carried his presence. Their gentleness carried his gentleness. Their crystal clarity carried his clarity. Even though my formal Zen training came through a fierce Korean lineage, the Zen I practiced in my heart — the Zen that quietly shaped the rhythms of my daily life — was profoundly influenced by Thích Nhất Hạnh and, in a parallel way, by the ancient master Mazu Daoyi.

The Pilgrimage to Huế

Then, after I retired and moved to Vietnam, Thầy passed away at his root temple in Huế, in January 2022.

His death felt strangely, deeply personal, as if a steady light had suddenly gone out in a familiar room I had lived in for years. About a year later, I made a quiet pilgrimage to Chùa Từ Hiếu. I walked the mossy grounds where he had walked as a teenage novice. I stood silently before the still pond where he had meditated through decades of memory. I breathed the exact same humid air he had breathed.

I didn't go there seeking a sign, an insight, or an experience. I went simply out of absolute gratitude. It remains one of the quietest, holiest moments of my life.

And yet, for all the books of his I have lived with, for all the teachings of his that have sculpted my mind, the one work that utterly changed the structural direction of my spiritual life was *Living Buddha, Living Christ*. It was not his historically deepest work, nor his most purely poetic, nor his most philosophically profound. But it was the precise document that gave me the ultimate permission to finally go home.

He wrote of Jesus Christ with such exquisite tenderness, such clarity, and such immense reverence that I felt something long-frozen inside me soften. He didn't clumsily attempt to merge Buddhism and Christianity into a hybrid doctrine. He simply showed how they beautifully reflect each other, like two ancient mirrors angled toward the exact same light.

Thầy taught me that returning to my Christian faith did not mean abandoning Zen. It meant discovering, with a shock of recognition, that Zen had been preparing me to understand Christianity all along.

He showed me that compassion is the ultimate meeting point of all great traditions. He showed me that mindfulness is a pure form of unceasing prayer. He showed me that God is intimately present in the arrival of every single breath.

Thích Nhất Hạnh was never just an author or a historical teacher to me; he was a living guide, a faithful companion, and a quiet, steady presence on the Mountain. He gave me permission to walk both paths. He gave me permission to integrate them within my own skin. He gave me permission to finally be whole.

And when I close my eyes and imagine the Mountain now, I see him there — walking slowly up the path, breathing gently, smiling with that soft, knowing, timeless smile. He is reminding me that enlightenment is never somewhere else.

It is here.

In this moment.

In this breath.

In this life.

CHAPTER SIX

Zen Master Seung Sahn: The Flawed Buddha Who Opened the Gate

When I first sought out a meditation teacher — after years of wandering through Pure Land practice and my own solitary experiments with Buddhism — I found myself in a Zen *sangha* deeply shaped by the direct teachings of Zen Master Seung Sahn. I didn't know it at the time, but that encounter would set the entire stage for my Zen education. Korean Zen was the very first Zen I ever knew, and Seung Sahn's voice became the first Zen voice that truly reached me.

Seung Sahn was born in 1927 in Korea, a resilient land marked by foreign occupation, devastating war, and profound cultural endurance. He became a monk at a young age, training in the exceptionally austere Korean Seon tradition. His practice was fierce, uncompromising, and deeply rooted in the ancient, iconoclastic lineage of Mazu Daoyi and Linji Yixuan. Eventually, he received Dharma transmission and made history as the first Korean Zen master to teach widely across the West.

He was a massive paradox in human form — part sudden thunderbolt, part warm teddy bear. A Korean *Budai* wielding a wooden Zen stick, he was a man whose booming laughter could instantly fill a room, and whose sudden shout could cut through complex delusion like a razor blade.

His foundational teaching was as simple as it was devastating:

"Only don't know."

That single phrase became the absolute ground beneath my feet. It was the first true koan I ever lived with, my very first taste of Zen's radical invitation to drop the armor of certainty and meet reality completely unfiltered.

Seung Sahn's teaching style was blunt, incredibly humorous, and utterly unpredictable. He utilized shouts, belly laughs, sharp paradoxes, and sudden, disruptive questions like a master craftsman handles his tools. He could be profoundly cosmic one moment and thoroughly ridiculous the next — and somehow, both movements were deep teachings.

Yet, what struck me most about Seung Sahn was not the lofty heights of his enlightenment. It was his raw, unvarnished humanity.

He was an openly flawed man — imperfect, impulsive, and at times controversial. And yet, his human flaws did not diminish his genuine wisdom an iota; if anything, they made it infinitely more accessible to an ordinary seeker like me. He showed me that true awakening does not require a pristine, stylized perfection. It requires absolute sincerity. He taught me that the Dharma can flow beautifully through cracked vessels, and that sometimes those very cracks are exactly what let the light pour through.

My own Zen lineage is intimately connected to his presence. My Dharma name, Min'ui Maitri, was given to me by one of his direct, former students. My current teacher, Myodo Jabo, likewise carries his lineage. Through them, Seung Sahn's distinct voice continues to echo loudly in my practice, in my own teaching, and in the exact way I approach koans and silent meditation.

It was through his specific line that I learned koan practice — not as an abstract intellectual puzzle to be solved by the brain, but as a living, embodied encounter with immediate reality. His approach to koans was direct, visceral, and thoroughly physical. He didn't want your clever explanations or your philosophical essays. He demanded a demonstration. He wanted you to show your understanding in the present moment, not talk about it.

This exact, no-nonsense approach heavily shaped my own teaching style and eventually became a significant part of my first book, *Sharing the Dharma*. His dynamic influence is woven through every one of those pages — the sharp humor, the directness, and the fierce insistence on internal sincerity over spiritual sophistication.

Seung Sahn taught me that awakening is never about becoming someone special. It's about finally becoming real. He taught me that the Mountain is climbed not by flawless, immaculate monks, but by ordinary, everyday people who are willing to look honestly and unflinchingly at their own messy minds. He taught me that wisdom can come beautifully wrapped in laughter, in stark contradiction, and in human imperfection.

And he taught me that true lineage is never about an obsessed concept of purity — it's about a living transmission, an authentic heart-to-heart connection, and the beautiful way a master's voice continues to echo through the lives and actions of their students.

When I close my eyes and imagine the Mountain now, I see Seung Sahn standing out on a rocky ridge — laughing, shouting, playfully waving his wooden stick, and demanding of me:

"What are you? Right now, tell me!"

And then he bursts into a booming laugh, because in the vast emptiness of the mountain, he already knows the answer.

He opened the gate for me. He set my feet firmly on the path. He showed me that true awakening is entirely possible within the borders of this flawed, chaotic, and beautiful life.

CHAPTER SEVEN

Bojo Jinul (Chinul): Sudden Awakening, Gradual Cultivation

Chinul came into my life not as a living, flesh-and-blood teacher, but as an intimate voice carried effortlessly across eight centuries — a Korean Seon master whose clarity still feels startlingly fresh. I never met him, of course. He lived from 1158 to 1210, long before Korea was a modern nation, long before Zen had crossed the vast ocean, and long before I ever sat on a cushion. And yet, when I finally encountered his ancient teachings, I felt as if he had been describing my exact path long before I ever knew I was walking it.

Chinul was born during the Goryeo dynasty, a historical epoch when Korean Buddhism had grown immensely wealthy, deeply political, and spiritually stagnant. As a young monk, he was utterly disillusioned by the systemic corruption he witnessed within the monasteries. He replication-longed for a radical return to authentic practice — to deep meditation, strict discipline, and the direct, unmediated experience of awakening. Consequently, he withdrew entirely from the corrupt institutional world and began gathering a small, dedicated community of monks who shared his inner longing.

What emerged from that intentional retreat was one of the most important, revolutionary insights in all of East Asian Zen history:

"Awakening is sudden. Cultivation is gradual."

This single, defining teaching became the foundational bedrock of the modern Jogye Order, the beating heart of Korean Seon, and — without my realizing it at first — the structural foundation of my own spiritual life.

When I first encountered Chinul's writing, I had already been practicing Zen for several years. I had experienced genuine moments of clarity, sudden flashes of insight, and real, fleeting glimpses of the Mountain's summit. But I had also discovered, much to my chagrin, that those profound moments did not magically transform my everyday life. They did not instantly erase my deep-seated habits, my stubborn ego, my lingering fears, or my personal flaws. The flashes of insight were real — but they were absolutely not the end of the road.

Chinul explained exactly why.

He taught that while awakening can happen in a single, timeless instant — a sudden, radical recognition of our true nature when the self falls away and reality shines through — that moment is merely the threshold. The rest of the journey — the long, slow, patient, and arduous work of embodying that pristine insight within our human skin — takes an entire lifetime.

When I read his words, I felt deeply seen. I felt understood, and I felt named. His teaching mirrored my exact dual experience: the sudden, spacious clarity of Zen practice followed by the long, gradual, and often messy work of living it out in daily life.

And it beautifully mirrored something else too — a truth from my Christian roots that I had not yet fully connected. St. James wrote, *"Faith without works is dead."* Chinul wrote, *"Awakening without cultivation is incomplete."* They were singing the exact same song in two entirely different keys.

Chinul taught me that enlightenment is never a trophy to be won. It is a profound responsibility.

He showed me that insight must become action, that clarity must transform into active compassion, and that awakening must empty itself into joyful service. He taught me that the Mountain is never climbed in a single, heroic leap, but step by step, breath by breath, and moment by painful moment.

In this specific way, Chinul stands directly beside St. John of the Cross on my Mountain — the medieval Korean Seon master and the sixteenth-century Spanish Carmelite mystic, both fiercely insisting that the spiritual path is simultaneously sudden and slow, luminous and laborious, an unmerited gift and a rigorous discipline.

Chinul gave me the map for my Zen life, and in doing so, he handed me the flawless map for my Catholic life. He taught me that:

— Grace can strike in an instant, but holiness is cultivated over years.

— Awakening is fully real, but transformation is entirely gradual.

— The Mountain is climbed not by a standard of perfection, but by pure perseverance.

When I close my eyes and imagine the Mountain now, I see Chinul standing quietly along the trail, his hands folded gently, watching the path ahead with a calm, knowing smile.

He doesn't shout like Seung Sahn.

He doesn't whisper like Thích Nhất Hạnh.

He simply stands there in the stillness, pointing with an open hand to the long, winding trail that climbs upward into the mist, saying:

"Awakening is sudden. The journey is lifelong."

And in that simple, beautiful teaching, he accurately described the entirety of my unfolding path — Zen and Catholic, East and West, sudden and gradual, faith and works, insight and transformation.

CHAPTER EIGHT

Jean-Pierre de Caussade: The Jesuit Who Showed Me That Zen Had Led Me Home

By the time I encountered Jean-Pierre de Caussade, I was already deep into Zen practice. I had sat countless hours on the cushion, wrestled with koans, received formal Dharma names, and lived inside the strict discipline of Korean Seon. On the cushion, I had awakened to the expansive present moment, learned how to let go of the heavy past, and stopped worrying about tomorrow. Zen had truly become the unshakeable ground beneath my feet.

And then, entirely unexpectedly, I met an eighteenth-century Jesuit priest who spoke Zen more fluently than many Zen teachers I had encountered.

De Caussade was born in 1675 in France, a Jesuit formed in the intense intellectual and meditative rigor of Ignatian spirituality. He spent a massive portion of his earthly life serving as a spiritual director to a quiet community of Visitation nuns — holy women who lived hidden, silent lives of unceasing prayer. He never traveled to Asia. He never read a single Buddhist sutra. He never sat *zazen* on a meditation cushion. And yet, somehow, he articulated the absolute essence of Zen with a crystal clarity that utterly startled me.

His practical teachings, preserved entirely in the ordinary letters these faithful nuns saved, were later compiled into the classic book *The Sacrament of the Present Moment*. When I first read those pages, I felt something massive inside my chest shift. It was as if a hidden door had suddenly swung open between two vast worlds I had long kept rigidly separate.

De Caussade taught that God is found not in dramatic visions or ecstasies, nor in spectacular, elite spiritual experiences, but exclusively in the simple duty of the present moment. He pointed to whatever is right before you. In the ordinary. In the now.

He wrote words that hit me like a familiar verse:

"The present moment holds infinite riches."

When I read that single line, I felt the unmistakable, deep resonance of Zen. It was "Chop wood, carry water" in a traditional Jesuit cassock. It was the realization that nirvana is found only in the present moment, spoken fluently in the ancient language of the Church.

But more than that — it was a radical revelation.

De Caussade showed me that Zen had never actually led me away from God. Zen had led me straight to Him. Everything I had laboriously learned on the cushion — letting go of the past, refusing to cling to the future, and awakening to the absolute present — was already dynamically present in the very heart of Christian Catholic mysticism.

De Caussade didn't pull me out of Zen. He met me directly inside my Zen practice, smiled, and whispered:

"This is where God has been waiting for you."

He taught me that every ordinary moment is an authentic sacrament — not just the Holy Eucharist, not just the formal liturgy, but the small, unremarkable moments that make up the fabric of a human life:

— washing the kitchen dishes

— walking down a quiet hallway

— listening intently to a friend

— sitting in absolute silence, breathing

He taught me that God is never elsewhere. God is here. Now. In this very breath.

And he taught me an insight that harmonized flawlessly with Chinul's deep teaching of sudden awakening and gradual cultivation:

Insight is sudden. Holiness is lived moment by moment.

This was St. James's declaration that "faith without works is dead," beautifully expressed through the lens of contemplative surrender. It was the exact same truth I had encountered in Zen: awakening is real, but it must be completely embodied in the ordinary, rhythmic habits of daily life.

De Caussade didn't just affirm my Zen practice. He baptized it. He sanctified it. He showed me that the God I had been seeking on the Mountain was not waiting at the peak.

He was waiting in the present moment.

When I close my eyes and imagine the Mountain now, I see de Caussade standing quietly near the path — not urging me upward, not demanding frantic progress, but reminding me with an open hand:

"This moment is enough. This moment is holy. This moment is God."

He was the Jesuit who showed me that Zen had not taken me away from my faith. Zen had perfectly prepared me to finally understand it.

CHAPTER NINE

Thomas Merton: The Trappist Who Showed Me the Bridge Was Always There

By the time I came to Thomas Merton, I had already walked far into Zen. I had sat with Vietnamese, Korean, and American teachers, wrestled with koans, received formal Dharma names, and lived inside the strict discipline of Seon. I had read Thích Nhất Hạnh, practiced mindfulness, and tasted the deep silence that Zen reveals. Yet, I still thought I was walking two entirely separate paths — one Eastern, one Western — and I wasn't sure how they were ever meant to fit together.

Then I met Merton.

Thomas Merton was born in 1915, a child of artists, a wanderer, and a restless seeker long before he ever knew the word "monk". His early life was heavily marked by profound loss; his mother died when he was only six years old, and his father passed away when he was sixteen. He drifted through Europe and America, searching for meaning in literature, philosophy, and the volatile energy of youth. And then, at the age of twenty-six, he walked into the Abbey of Gethsemani in Kentucky and never looked back.

He became a Trappist monk — a choir monk, a contemplative, a man who prayed seven times a day in the ancient rhythm of the monastic hours. But he was also a writer, a global thinker, and a brilliant spirit who refused to let the cloister walls close him off from the world. His autobiography, *The Seven Storey Mountain*, made him instantly famous, but it was his later writings — the raw journals, the essays, the letters — that truly revealed the immense depth of his contemplative heart.

And it was in those exact, mature writings that he discovered Zen.

Merton never pretended to be a Zen master. He never claimed a spectacular enlightenment. But he recognized something in Zen that resonated flawlessly with the deepest currents of Christian mysticism — the apophatic silence of John of the Cross, the luminous emptiness of Meister Eckhart, and the absolute contemplative stillness of the Desert Fathers.

When Merton read D.T. Suzuki, he felt a sudden shock of recognition. When he met Thích Nhất Hạnh, he felt an immediate, spiritual brotherhood. When he wrote about Zen, he did so with deep reverence, immense humility, and total clarity.

Merton taught me that the contemplative heart is entirely universal.

He showed me that the vast silence I found on the meditation cushion was the exact same silence he found in the choir stalls of Gethsemani. He showed me that the emptiness I encountered in Zen was never foreign to Christianity — it was already dynamically present in its mystical core. He showed me that the Mountain I was climbing had many paths, but only one summit.

Merton didn't lazily collapse East and West into each other. He honored their distinct differences. But he also clearly saw their shared center.

He wrote words that made me pause:

"There is no East and no West. There is only the dance."

When I read those words, something turbulent in me finally settled. I realized I wasn't walking two conflicting paths at all. I was walking one single path with two languages.

Merton helped me see that my Zen practice was never a departure from my Catholic faith. It was a deepening of it. A widening of it. A pure, unadulterated purification of it.

He taught me that:

Contemplation is not about escaping the world, but about seeing it clearly.

— Silence is not an empty void, but an absolute fullness.

— God is never found in rigid concepts, but in direct, unmediated experience.

And he taught me something else — an essential truth that perfectly prepared me for the final synthesis of my own unfolding journey:

The true contemplative is always a beginner.

When I close my eyes and imagine the Mountain now, I see Merton standing somewhere right between the East and the West, smiling with that quiet, knowing, timeless smile of his. He is holding out an open hand to both sides, saying:

"Come. There is room for everyone in the silence."

He was the monk who showed me that the bridge between Zen and Catholicism was not something I had to exhaustively build.

It was already there. I simply had to walk across it.

CHAPTER TEN

Mazu Daoyi: The Thunderous Ancestor Who Twisted My Nose Awake

Mazu Daoyi came into my life the way he came into many people's lives — not as a gentle guide, but as a pure shock. A jolt. A shout across the centuries. I never met him, of course. He lived in eighth-century China, long before Korea shaped the Zen I first encountered in the West. But through the raw stories preserved in the Chan tradition — the nose-twisting, the shouts, the impossible questions — Mazu became one of the foundational ancestors who shaped my Zen heart.

Mazu was born in 709 in what is now the Sichuan Province. He trained under Nanyue Huairang, who was himself a direct student of the legendary Sixth Patriarch, Huineng. Mazu's early years were heavily marked by intense, exhausting practice — long hours of silent meditation, fierce discipline, and a relentless drive to awaken. But what ultimately made him a legend across the centuries was not his quiet piety. It was his thunderous teaching style.

Mazu taught like a sudden thunderstorm.

He shouted.

He struck.

He twisted noses.

He asked impossible questions.

He shattered human concepts with the absolute force of a sledgehammer.

One of the first stories of Mazu that reached me was the famous exchange with his teacher, Nanyue. Mazu had been sitting in solitary meditation for years, fiercely trying to become a Buddha.

Recognizing his delusion, Nanyue quietly picked up a clay tile brick near him and began polishing it on a stone.

When Mazu asked what he was doing, Nanyue replied:

"I am polishing this brick to make a mirror."

Mazu protested, "How can polishing a brick ever make a mirror?"

Nanyue instantly shot back:

"How can sitting in meditation ever make a Buddha?"

That ancient story hit me like a physical koan thrown straight at my forehead. It was the first time I understood — truly and deeply understood — that authentic Zen is never about striving to become something else. It is about finally seeing what is already entirely true.

Another famous story that shaped my early practice was an exchange where a traveling monk asked Mazu, "What is Buddha?"

Mazu replied directly:

"Mind is Buddha."

Later, another seeker approached him and asked the exact same question. This time, Mazu looked at him and replied:

"No mind, no Buddha."

Those two answers — utterly contradictory on the logical surface — were the sharpest spiritual teaching I had ever encountered. They taught me that Zen is never about clinging to a safe, static doctrine. It is about fearlessly meeting the present moment. It is about responding from mirror-deep clarity, not from safe memory. It is about total freedom.

Mazu's raw teachings reached me across the centuries through the lineage of Korean Seon I first practiced in. Zen Master Seung Sahn's abrupt shouts, his striking stick, his sudden, destabilizing questions — all of that wild medicine came straight from Mazu. The entire flavor of Korean Seon is deeply steeped in Mazu's fierce, uncompromising compassion. Even the concrete koan practice I learned — the direct, completely embodied, *show-me-your-mind* approach — carries his unmistakable fingerprints.

And in a beautiful, strange paradox, Mazu perfectly prepared me for the gentleness of Thích Nhất Hạnh. He prepared me for the systematic clarity of Chinul. He prepared me for the present-moment sacrament of de Caussade, and the luminous simplicity of Thomas Aquinas.

He did this because Mazu taught me something absolutely essential:

— Awakening is not polite.

— Awakening is not tidy.

— Awakening is not conceptual.

— Awakening is direct, immediate, unfiltered, and alive.

Mazu taught me that the Mountain is never climbed by thinking about it. It is climbed exclusively by stepping into the present moment with your total, unreserved presence.

He showed me that the Dharma is not a fragile thing to be protected. It can shout. It can twist your nose awake. It can completely break your treasured religious ideas so that your heart can finally open to grace.

When I close my eyes and imagine the Mountain now, I see Mazu standing somewhere near the steepest, most precipitous part of the trail — laughing, shouting, pointing into the abyss, challenging me, and utterly refusing to let me settle for a safe, conceptual understanding of God or emptiness.

He is the ancestor who looks me in the eyes and commands:

*"Don't polish the brick. Don't chase the Buddha. Show me your true nature —
right now."*

Mazu was the raw thunder in my lineage. He was the jolt that woke
me up. He was the fierce, loving ancestor who taught me that
awakening is never something you think about.

It is something you live.

CHAPTER ELEVEN

The Permission Givers

Every spiritual journey has its gatekeepers — not the kind who bar the way, but the kind who quietly open a door you didn't know you were allowed to walk through. They don't give you cheap answers. They give you permission.

Permission to trust your own sincerity.

Permission to follow the hidden thread of your longing.

Permission to take the next trembling step toward the Mountain.

For me, three distinct teachers offered that crucial permission at three different thresholds: Myodo Jabo, Thích Nhất Hạnh, and Thomas Merton. Each one appeared at exactly the right moment in my life. Each one spoke the same underlying truth in a different tongue, and each one beautifully widened the path beneath my feet.

Myodo Jabo — The First Permission: *"Your intentions are pure."*

I first met Myodo Jabo in 2015, at a time when my Buddhist practice was shifting frantically beneath my feet. I had been deeply immersed in Pure Land practice for years, but the *nembutsu* repetition alone was no longer enough. Meditation had become my absolute refuge from PTSD — the one safe place where my mind could finally breathe. I desperately needed a master who could guide me deeper into that silence.

That was when I found Myodo — and, almost simultaneously, a Sri Lankan Theravada monk who welcomed me into his own historical lineage. For several years I walked what I jokingly called my years of "Saffron Zen" — a dual practice of Korean Seon and Theravada insight meditation. It was an unusual, hybrid path, but it felt right. Both traditions steadied me, and both gave me tools I desperately needed to survive my internal landscapes.

But around 2018, something deep inside me shifted. I intellectualized the path and convinced myself that Theravada was the only "real Buddhism," the pure, original form of the elders. Zen suddenly felt too poetic, too paradoxical, and too wild. So, I left Myodo's *sangha* and committed my life entirely to the Theravada temple. I became a formal Dharma teacher for children. I taught them the Five Precepts, the Four Noble Truths, and the Eightfold Path. I bowed to the Buddha in Sinhala, chanted the refuges in Pali, and tried with all my might to make the temple my permanent home.

And for a while, it worked.

But then, in 2021, during a deep meditation at the temple, something entirely unexpected happened. I was contemplating the traditional path of the *Arhat* — liberation exclusively for oneself — when a realization rose up within my chest with the striking force of a massive bronze bell:

"I cannot be free while others suffer."

It wasn't born of religious guilt, and it wasn't born of Buddhist doctrine. It was *bodhicitta* — the raw mind of awakening — blooming in my chest like a sudden, brilliant sunrise. In that single moment, I realized that what I had been seeking all those years was never "the religion of Buddhism". It was non-duality. It was the ultimate path where personal awakening and universal compassion are the exact same breath. It was the vow to help all sentient beings up the mountain, not just myself.

And I knew exactly where I needed to go.

I reached out to Myodo again — hesitant, deeply humbled, almost on bended knee. I explicitly told her I wanted to return to Zen, but I wasn't sure if I was even allowed back. I had left her. I had wandered. I had been wrong.

She listened to my confession entirely quietly, then looked at me with the immense, spacious clarity that only comes from decades of dedicated practice, and said:

"Min'ui, there are many paths up the mountain as long as your intentions are pure."

That single sentence was my first real, embodied lesson in non-duality. She wasn't lazily telling me that all religious traditions are identical. She was telling me that internal sincerity is infinitely deeper than external tradition. That the Mountain is always larger than any human map, and that the heart ultimately knows its own way.

Her profound permission didn't simply welcome me back to a Zen hall. It welcomed me back to myself. It affirmed the *bodhicitta* that had shattered my isolation, and it validated the path of compassion I could no longer ignore. Only through *bodhicitta* was I going to find the peace I was seeking; only through non-duality could I walk the Mountain with absolute integrity. Myodo didn't just give me permission to return. She gave me permission to be whole.

Thích Nhất Hạnh — The Second Permission: *"You can go home."*

When I first read *Living Buddha, Living Christ,* something hardened in me softened in a way I hadn't anticipated. Thích Nhất Hạnh didn't clumsily blur Buddhism and Christianity together into a generic philosophy. He didn't try to make them identical. Instead, he showed how the deepest, mystical truths of both traditions reflect each other perfectly, like two mirrors angled toward the exact same source of light.

And then, he did something truly astonishing for an Eastern master. He gave me permission to go home.

He didn't mean back to my unexamined childhood beliefs or rigid dogma, but back to the living, contemplative roots of my own heart. Thầy taught me that returning to Christianity did not require me to abandon Zen. It meant discovering that Zen had been preparing me to finally receive Christianity all along.

He beautifully expanded Myodo's teaching that the Mountain has many paths, adding a new, comforting dimension: some paths are meant to lead you right back to where you began, but equipped with entirely new eyes. Without Thích Nhất Hạnh, I would never have given Catholicism a second chance. He was the one who looked at my split life and said: *"You can go home, and you can bring your Zen with you."*

Thomas Merton — The Third Permission: *"You are not alone on this path."*

By the time I fully discovered Thomas Merton, I had already begun quietly exploring the Christian contemplative tradition — the Rule of St. Benedict, the rhythm of monastic prayer, and the quiet depth of *Lectio Divina*. And to my utter surprise, *Lectio Divina* felt uncannily, structurally identical to Zen. I watched the movements align perfectly:

— *Lectio* (the slow, attentive reading) mirrored Zen's initial settling of the body.

— *Meditatio* (the slow "chewing" of a sacred word) mirrored the exact way a koan completely exhausts the analytical mind.

— *Oratio* (the spontaneous opening of the heart) mirrored Zen's profound compassionate intention.

— *Contemplatio* (the wordless, silent resting in God) mirrored the objectless awareness of *zazen*.

I began to see clearly that East and West were not historical opposites. They were the two wings of the exact same bird.

But I still desperately needed reassurance. Was I actually allowed to practice Zen and still remain a faithful, devout Catholic? Was I dangerously wandering off the path? Was I becoming a bizarre hybrid, something fundamentally suspect to the Church?

Merton answered those exact questions centuries before I could ask them. He had walked this precise terrain long before me. He had corresponded extensively with D.T. Suzuki, met Thích Nhất Hạnh face-to-face, and explicitly called him "my brother." He recognized that the contemplative heart is entirely universal.

Merton didn't give me permission to abandon anything. He gave me permission to integrate. He told me, through his journals and essays: *"You are not a bad Catholic for practicing Zen. You are a contemplative walking the same mountain path I walked."* His writings became a map I could trust, and his life became a steady reassurance that I was never alone.

Three Permissions, One Path

Spiritual learning is a spiral; we are often required to hear the exact same truth over and over at different waypoints until it finally sinks into the marrow of our bones. Looking back across the years of my wandering, the pattern reveals itself with perfect clarity:

— Myodo Jabo gave me permission to change paths.

— Thích Nhất Hạnh gave me permission to go home.

— Thomas Merton gave me permission to integrate the two.

Three distinct teachers. Three unique thresholds. Three necessary steps toward the Mountain. Each one taught me the exact same lesson at a different juncture of my life:

The Mountain is one.

The paths are many.

Walk with absolute sincerity, and you will never be lost.

CHAPTER TWELVE

The Mountain

There is a sacred place in the spiritual imagination where traditions meet without colliding, where ancient truths echo each other without losing a fraction of their distinct tones. For me, that place has always been the Mountain.

In Korean Seon, the Mountain is never a mere metaphor. It is a living teacher.

Mountains are the precise landscapes where monasteries were built, where masters endured, and where radical awakening happened. Mountains are where silence matures into a physical presence, where dramatic distance transforms into mirror-deep clarity, and where the mind effortlessly empties itself simply by looking out across the vast, rolling ridgelines.

The writer David Hinton notes that mountains possess a "resounding silence," a stark clarity that perfectly mirrors the empty mind. When I first encountered that phrase, I realized with a shock of recognition that the Mountain had been the silent, faithful companion of my own journey long before I ever possessed the words to name it.

And it is on this Korean Mountain — this Seon landscape of silence and absolute clarity — that I imagine a timeless gathering, a meeting of the greatest teachers of my life.

Silence and Simplicity

RAMBAM, the great Jewish philosopher, would have felt completely at home on these rocky ridges. His rigorous apophatic theology — the fierce insistence that God can only be truly known by what God is not — is the flawless intellectual cousin of Zen's emptiness.

In the quiet of the high altitude, I imagine RAMBAM standing peacefully, looking out over the deep, mist-covered valleys, and whispering into the wind:

"The closer you come to the Divine, the fewer words you can use."

And the Mountain answers him seamlessly with its own boundless silence. Zen calls it emptiness; RAMBAM calls it simplicity. Both terms point directly toward the exact same ungraspable Reality.

As they stand there, Thomas Aquinas slowly ascends the trail. He climbs the Mountain with heavy books weighted in his pack — Aristotle, ancient Scripture, and the pages of the *Summa* half-written in his brilliant mind. But as he gains elevation, the air thins. Rigid concepts begin to loosen. Complex scholastic arguments simply fall away into the brush.

At the summit, he experiences his final, quiet vision — the one that made him permanently lay down his inkwell, the one that made him declare that all he had written seemed like mere straw. On the Mountain, Aquinas finally sheds the philosopher and becomes entirely a mystic.

He stands quietly beside RAMBAM. Both of them gaze directly into the same luminous simplicity, both intimately realizing that the human intellect can only carry you so far up the rock face. Beyond that sharp point, only silence remains.

The Sudden and the Slow

John of the Cross arrives at the summit entirely differently. He doesn't spend his energy climbing; he simply emerges.

He steps directly out of the dark night like a man who has walked completely through a furnace fire and discovered it to be pure light. His haunting, Spanish refrain — *nada, nada, nada* — echoes across the open stone of the Mountain like a live koan.

He looks at RAMBAM and Aquinas, smiles warmly, and says:

"To come to the All, you must go by way of nothing."

And the Mountain gently nods its agreement. Zen calls it emptiness; John calls it *nada*. Both are beautiful, spacious doorways leading into the exact same luminous dark.

Beside the Carmelite stands Chinul, the grand synthesizer of Korean Seon. He is the ancient master who maps the rhythm of sudden awakening and gradual cultivation. He knows with absolute certainty that grace and enlightenment can strike a life like sudden lightning, but that actually living it out takes an entire lifetime of patience.

On the ridge, Chinul looks at John of the Cross and observes:

"Awakening is sudden. Sanctification is gradual."

John smiles broadly. He has been teaching his own friars the exact same truth for centuries. I hear their voices intertwine in the breeze, and I finally understand.

Twin Guardians of Mercy

And then — in the most unexpected and yet entirely natural moment of the vision — two figures appear who are not philosophers, not theologians, and not monks, but pure presences.

The Blessed Virgin Mary and Avalokiteshvara, whom my heart knows as Quan Yin, the Bodhisattva of Compassion. They stand hand-in-hand upon the grass like twin guardians of mercy.

Mary, that magnificent, living Ark of the Covenant, whose quiet *fiat* opened the fragile fabric of the world to host the eternal Word. And Quan Yin, whose thousand outstretched arms reach tirelessly into every dark corner of human suffering.

They look at me — not with an ounce of institutional judgment, but with the gentlest, most piercing recognition. They look at my scars, my detours, and my heavy pacing, and they say in unison:

"You don't have to climb so fast, Tom. There are many others you can help along the way."

And suddenly, with those words, the Mountain ceases to be a lonely place of spiritual escape. It transforms into a place of active return.

Ad Iesum per Mariam. To Jesus through Mary. And Quan Yin adds, in her own exquisitely thunderous way:

"Min'ui, I hear their cries. Do you hear them too? Return and help them."

Two ancient traditions. One single compassion. One majestic Mountain.

How to Walk

Standing on this high peak, surrounded by this silent chorus, the Mountain finally teaches me how to walk:

Awakening is real.

Cultivation is lifelong.

Silence is a teacher.

Compassion is the path.

God is simple.

Emptiness is luminous.

The Christian saints and the Buddhist bodhisattvas are not rivals fighting for the peak. The Mountain itself belongs exclusively to no single human tradition; it belongs entirely to all who sincerely seek.

And across the ridgeline, I hear again the ancient Seon teaching that has reliably guided my steps through the darkness for decades:

You can see the Mountain from the North as well as from the South.

The paths wind upward from entirely different directions, but the Mountain itself — the silence, the clarity, the vast presence — is one.

CHAPTER THIRTEEN

The Names We Are Given

Every spiritual tradition deeply understands that names are never merely arbitrary labels. They are invitations.

In ancient Scripture, receiving a new name always signals a profound, un-turnable turning point in the soul:

— Abram becomes Abraham, the father of nations.

— Jacob becomes Israel, the one who wrestles with God.

— Saul becomes Paul, the apostle who sees reality with entirely new eyes.

A new name is never a cosmetic change. It signals a radical shift in identity — or more precisely, a complete shift in the exact way identity is held. Zen carries this same ancient, deep intuition. A Dharma name is not a definition of who you are. It is a living call toward who you are called to become.

I have been given three specific names in my life that have uniquely shaped my path up the Mountain:

— my Christian name, Thomas

— my Vietnamese Dharma name, Quang Phúc Lạc

— my Korean Dharma name, Min'ui Maitri

Each one arrived at a completely different juncture of my life. Each one revealed a distinct facet of the inner terrain, and each one eventually transformed from a label into a lifelong practice.

The First Path: Thomas

My Christian name was the very first spiritual gift spoken over my life — a name deeply rooted in the ancient communion of saints, the long story of the Church, and the water-washed mystery of baptism. But "Thomas" is not a simple, single-layered name. It carries an intricate constellation of meanings.

First, there is Thomas the Apostle — the one historically branded as the doubter, but who was, in truth, the one who demanded to touch. He fiercely refused to accept a secondhand truth. He replication-longed for a direct, unmediated experience, requiring his own hand to enter the physical wound. That immediate, unarmored demand is the very heart of Zen.

Then, there is Thomas Aquinas — the towering mind who climbed the massive ladder of human reason. He sought absolute clarity, structural coherence, and deep understanding. And yet, at the very summit of his intellectual ascent, he let the ladder go, declaring everything he had written to be like straw. That surrender is the exact deployment of the Buddha's raft.

Finally, there is Thomas More — the individual conscience that stands entirely unmoveable. He resolutely refused to betray internal truth for external comfort, perfectly embodying a compassionate justice with an iron spine. That particular manifestation was my ultimate Dharma name, quietly waiting across decades to be spoken aloud.

These three Thomases do not define a fixed, separate "self." Rather, they illuminate the dynamic terrain of my journey: the seeker, the thinker, and the conscience. They were my very first reliable guides up the Mountain.

The Radiant Seed: Quang Phúc Lạc

My first Zen Master, Thich Đạo Quang, looked at me and handed me my Vietnamese Dharma name: *Quang Phúc Lạc*. Ideographically written as 光福樂, it translates to a beautiful invocation: *Blessed Joy. Blissful Merit. The deep happiness that arises exclusively from goodness.*

This name was never an accurate description of who I was at the time. It was an aspiration — a clear, spiritual direction. It pointed my eyes toward:

— the deep joy that naturally comes from awakening

— the profound ease that arises when the tight grip of the self finally loosens

— the unshakeable bliss that is completely independent of external circumstances

— the inner radiance that comes from living in absolute harmony with the Dharma

This name planted the very first seed of my contemplative life. It constantly whispered into the noise of my mind: *"Joy is not something you frantically chase. It is something you quietly uncover."* It was my first true hint that God could be found within emptiness, that silence could be luminous, and that true bliss could arise from a radical letting go.

The Iron Spine: Min'ui Maitri

Later, as my practice deepened within the discipline of Korean Seon, I received my second Dharma name: *Min'ui Maitri.* My *Soensanim* translated its core meaning as *Compassionate Justice.*

This name was not soft. It was razor-sharp, highly active, and exceptionally demanding. My teacher delivered it with a very traditional, theatrical Korean Zen flourish. He locked his eyes onto mine and commanded:

"Min'ui, show me Compassionate Justice."

He did not ask me to define it with words, or explain its mechanics in an essay. He demanded that I show it. In the Korean tradition, a

Dharma name is never a title to wear; it is an active role you must fully inhabit — a living koan you are required to become.

This name pointed my life toward a new, demanding landscape:

— compassion backed by a clear backbone

— justice rooted deeply in mercy

— the seamless union of Quan Yin and Jesus Christ

— the immediate courage to act

— the painful tenderness required to truly listen

— the total willingness to stand directly with those who suffer

It was the precise name that echoed the unyielding stance of Thomas More. It was the name that structurally prepared my heart to meet Mary and Avalokiteshvara on the ridge. It was the name that taught me, once and for all, that true awakening can never be passive. Compassion must move. Justice must breathe.

Mandalas of the Heart

In the light of the Dharma, names never define a solid, unmoving self. Instead, they beautifully reveal the ultimate emptiness of the self. They demonstrate that identity is never a fixed cage, but is fluid, relational, and deeply aspirational.

My Christian name intimately ties me to Christ, to Mary, and to the global communion of saints. My Vietnamese name ties me to joy, to merit, and to the spacious bliss of awakening. My Korean name ties me to compassion, to justice, and to the active vow to help others up the Mountain. Together, they form a perfect mandala — a map of the path I have walked, and the path I am still walking today.

On the Mountain — that Seon landscape where RAMBAM, Aquinas, John of the Cross, and Chinul all meet in council — I imagine these three names meeting as well.

Thomas the Apostle reaches out and touches the physical wound. Thomas Aquinas steps back and lets go of his ladder. Thomas More stands firm in absolute conscience. *Quang Phúc Lạc* radiates an uncaused joy, while *Min'ui Maitri* acts with fierce compassion.

And then Mary and Avalokiteshvara step forward — the Mother and the Bodhisattva — and they say to me again:

"You don't have to climb so fast, Tom. There are many others you can help along the way."

In the silence that follows, I hear Christ whisper: *"When you have done it unto the least of these, you have done it unto me."* And I hear the ancient *Heart Sutra* respond: *"Form is emptiness, emptiness is form."*

And I finally realize the truth. My names are not identities to protect. They are vocations. They are the path itself.

CHAPTER FOURTEEN

The Insight of St. John of the Cross: The Practice Manual

I did not come to *The Dark Night of the Soul* as an academic scholar, or as a casual reader browsing the classic anthologies of Christian literature. I came to it as a man who had already spent fifteen years sitting silently on a zafu cushion, watching thoughts rise and fall, and learning to systematically let go of every mental image of self and God that crossed the mind. By the time I met Juan de la Cruz on the page, I believed I had already walked through my own ultimate dark nights. I knew silence; I knew emptiness; I knew unknowing.

And then I read his words, and realized I had only been standing at the absolute edge of the abyss.

St. John of the Cross does not write about the dark night as a distant, abstract idea. He writes entirely from within it. The poem and its subsequent commentaries are not theology in the abstract; they are a direct, raw field report from the hidden interior of total surrender. The true "dark night" he describes is not clinical depression, it is not intellectual doubt, and it is certainly not God's absence. It is God's overwhelming presence in a form the fragile ego cannot recognize. It is the unadulterated light of the Divine shining so blindingly bright that, to our ordinary, limited way of seeing, it can only appear as total darkness.

What struck me first about his manual was how incredibly practical it all was. For all its exquisite literary beauty, *The Dark Night* is, at its core, a manual for practice. John describes, with almost clinical, step-by-step precision, how God strips the soul of its lingering attachments:

— first to raw sensory consolations

— then to subtle spiritual consolations

— and finally, even to its own treasured, conceptual ideas of God

He walks the reader patiently through the stages of letting go — of images, of feelings, of concepts — until the soul stands completely naked before the One it cannot name. It is never a path of addition, but of absolute subtraction.

And then there was that single, resonant word: *nada*. Nothing, nothing, nothing.

The more I lived with that word, the more that Spanish refrain began to echo the *Heart Sutra* in my own mind. *"Nada, nada, nada"* sounded uncannily like *"no eye, no ear, no tongue..."* The sixteenth-century Spanish Carmelite and the ancient Mahayana sutra were singing the exact same song of liberation in two different keys. John's apophatic theology — his fierce insistence that God is reached exclusively not by what we say, but by what we relinquish — felt like a Christian baptism of the very emptiness I had been practicing for over a decade in Zen.

For me, *The Dark Night of the Soul* became the Catholic face of a mountain I already intimately knew from the Buddhist side. It showed me that what I had learned in *zazen* — the constant letting go of self, of concepts, of psychological grasping — was already present in the mystical heart of my own tradition. John was not leading me away from Zen. He was meeting me directly inside the same luminous darkness and naming it God.

Here is his poem — a true practice manual for perfect wisdom.

Noche Oscura del Alma

I

En una noche oscura,

con ansias, en amores inflamada,

¡oh dichosa ventura!,

salí sin ser notada

estando ya mi casa sosegada.

In a dark night,

Ablaze with the anxieties of love,

Oh, fortunate venture!

I went out unseen,

My house being now at peace.

II

A oscuras y segura,

por la secreta escala, disfrazada,

¡oh dichosa ventura!,

a oscuras y en celada,

estando ya mi casa sosegada.

In darkness and secure,

By the secret ladder, disguised,

Oh, fortunate venture!

In darkness and under cover,

My house being now at peace.

III

En la noche dichosa,

en secreto, que nadie me veía,

ni yo miraba cosa,

sin otra luz y guía

sino la que en el corazón ardía.

In that fortunate night,

In secret, for no one saw me,

Nor did I look at anything,

With no other light or guide

Than the one burning in my heart.

IV

Aquésta me guiaba

más cierto que la luz del mediodía,

adonde me esperaba

quien yo bien me sabía,

en parte donde nadie parecía.

This light guided me

More surely than the midday sun,

To where the one I knew so well

Was waiting for me—

In a place where no one else appeared.

V

¡Oh noche que guiaste!,

¡oh noche amable más que el alborada!,

¡oh noche que juntaste

Amado con amada,

amada en el Amado transformada!

Oh night that guided me!

Oh night more lovely than the dawn!

Oh night that joined

The Beloved with the beloved,

The beloved transformed into the Beloved!

VI

En mi pecho florido,

que entero para él solo se guardaba,

allí quedó dormido,

y yo le regalaba,

y el ventalle de cedros aire daba.

Upon my flowering breast,

Kept entirely for him alone,

There he fell asleep,

And I caressed him,

While the fanning of the cedros gave us air.

VII

El aire de la almena,

cuando yo sus cabellos esparcía,

con su mano serena

en mi cuello hería,

y todos mis sentidos suspendía.

The breeze from the turret,

As I scattered his hair,

Wounded my neck

With its serene hand,

Suspending all my senses.

VIII

Quedéme y olvidéme,

el rostro recliné sobre el Amado;

cesó todo y dejéme,

dejando mi cuidado

entre las azucenas olvidado.

I abandoned myself and forgot myself,

Resting my face upon the Beloved;

All ceased, and I let myself go,

Leaving my cares

Forgotten among the lilies.

“He must increase, but I must decrease.”
John 3:30 (Douay–Rheims)

CHAPTER FIFTEEN

The Perfection of Wisdom Heart Sutra: The Practice Manual

I did not come to the *Heart Sutra* as an academic scholar of
Buddhism. I came to it as someone who had spent years sitting in
deep silence, watching the separate self dissolve and reassemble, and
learning to gradually trust the vast space between thoughts. I had
chanted the liturgy for years, but by the time I intimately understood
its core, I had already lived inside the discipline of Zen long enough
to know that its deepest teachings are rarely found in intellectual
explanations. They are found exclusively in the places where human
language completely collapses.

The *Heart Sutra* is the shortest scripture in Mahayana Buddhism, but
it cuts the deepest. It is not a philosophical treatise; it is not a
complex metaphysical argument. It is a direct set of instructions for
seeing cleanly through the illusion of a separate self. It is a manual
for walking straight into emptiness and discovering that emptiness
is not a stark void, but a luminous fullness too vast for the analytical
mind to ever grasp.

When the Bodhisattva Avalokiteshvara "looked deeply into the five
skandhas and saw that they are empty," he was not performing an
objective intellectual analysis. He was describing the exact moment
the heavy scaffolding of the ego falls away. It is the moment when
the mind finally stops clinging to form, feeling, perception, impulse,
and consciousness as if they were solid, unchanging realities. It is the
moment when reality is suddenly seen as it truly is: fluid,
interdependent, and beautifully ungraspable.

And then comes the line that has echoed loudly through Zen halls
for centuries:

"Form is emptiness, emptiness is form."

For years, I chanted those words without fully understanding them
within my own skin. I thought they were merely deep paradox, high
poetry, or oriental philosophy. But the more I practiced on the
cushion, the more I realized they were concrete instructions. They

were telling me exactly how to see. They were telling me how to let go. They were showing me that the world is never divided into rigid binaries of sacred and profane, self and other, or God and creation. Everything is interwoven. Everything is empty of separate existence, and therefore, everything is completely full of everything else.

Following this realization comes the great, sweeping negation:

"No eye, no ear, no tongue…"

This is never nihilism. It is absolute liberation. It is the systematic stripping away of every single category the grasping mind uses to manipulate and partition reality. This is the Buddhist version of apophatic theology — the radical refusal to let any concept, any image, or any mental idea stand in for the unnameable Truth. It is the exact same interior movement John of the Cross describes when he whispers *"nada, nada, nada."* The same surrender. The same luminous dark.

For me, the *Heart Sutra* became the Buddhist face of a mountain I had originally begun climbing as a child from the Christian side. It showed me that the emptiness I encountered in Zen was never a cold rejection of God, but a thorough purification of the fragile self that tries to domesticate and grasp God. It showed me that the silence I found on the cushion was the exact same silence the Christian mystics uncovered in their cloistered cells. It showed me that the Mountain has only one summit, even if the paths wind upward from completely different directions.

The *Heart Sutra* did not lead me away from Christianity. It perfectly prepared me to finally understand it.

Here is the complete sutra in Chinese and English.

The Heart of the Perfection of Wisdom Sutra

摩訶般若波羅蜜多心經
mo hé bō rě bō luó mì duō xīn jīng
觀自在菩薩行深般若
guān zì zài pú sà xíng shēn bō rě
波羅蜜多時照見五蘊皆空
bō luó mì duō shí zhào jiàn wǔ yùn jiē kōng
度一切苦厄
dù yī qiè kǔ è
舍利子色不異空
shě lì zǐ sè bù yì kōng
空不異色色即是空
kōng bù yì sè sè jí shì kōng
空即是色
kōng jí shì sè
受想行識亦復如是
shòu xiǎng xíng shí yì fù rú shì
舍利子是諸法空相
shě lì zǐ shì zhū fǎ kōng xiàng
不生不滅不垢不淨
bù shēng bù miè bù gòu bù jìng
不增不減是故空中無色
bù zēng bù jiǎn shì gù kōng zhōng wú sè
無受想行識無眼耳鼻舌身意
wú shòu xiǎng xíng shí wú yǎn ěr bí shé shēn yì
無色聲香味觸法
wú sè shēng xiāng wèi chù fǎ
無眼界乃至無意識界
wú yǎn jiè nǎi zhì wú yì shí jiè
無無明亦無無明盡
wú wú míng yì wú wú míng jìn
乃至無老死亦無老死盡
nǎi zhì wú lǎo sǐ yì wú lǎo sǐ jìn
無苦集滅道無智亦無得以

wú kǔ jí miè dào wú zhì yì wú dé yǐ

無所得故菩提薩埵依

wú suǒ dé gù pú tí sà duǒ yī

般若波羅蜜多故心無罣礙

bō rě bō luó mì duō gù xīn wú guà ài

無罣礙故無有恐怖

wú guà ài gù wú yǒu kǒng bù

遠離一切顛倒夢想究竟

yuǎn lí yī qiè diān dǎo mèng xiǎng jiū jìng

涅槃三世諸佛依般若

niè pán sān shì zhū fó yī bō rě

波羅蜜多故得阿耨多羅

bō luó mì duō gù dé ā nòu duō luó

三藐三菩提故知般若

sān miǎo sān pú tí gù zhī bō rě

波羅蜜多是大神呪

bō luó mì duō shì dà shén zhòu

是大明呪是無上呪

shì dà míng zhòu shì wú shàng zhòu

是無等等呪能除一切苦

shì wú děng děng zhòu néng chú yī qiè kǔ

眞實不虛故說般若波羅蜜多

zhēn shí bù xū gù shuō bō rě bō luó mì duō

呪即說呪曰

zhòu jí shuō zhòu yuē

揭諦揭諦波羅揭諦波羅僧揭諦菩提娑婆訶

jiē dì jiē dì bō luó jiē dì bō luó sēng jiē dì pú tí suō pó hē

English Translation

When the Bodhisattva Avalokiteshvara was practicing deep Prajñāpāramitā (the Perfection of Wisdom [meditation]), he illuminated the Five Skandhas (components of existence) and saw that they are all empty, thereby overcoming all suffering and distress.

"Shariputra, **form is not different from emptiness, emptiness is not different from form; form is emptiness, emptiness is form.** The same is true of feelings, perceptions, impulses, and consciousness."

"Shariputra, all phenomena are marked with emptiness; they are neither born nor destroyed, neither defiled nor pure, neither increasing nor decreasing. Therefore, in emptiness there is no form, no feeling, perception, impulse, or consciousness."

"No eye, ear, nose, tongue, body, or mind; no color, sound, smell, taste, touch, or phenomena. No realm of sight, and so on, down to no realm of consciousness."

"There is no ignorance, and no end to ignorance, and so on, down to no old age and death, and no end to old age and death."

"There is no suffering, no cause of suffering, no cessation of suffering, and no path. There is no wisdom, and no attainment, because there is nothing to be attained."

"The Bodhisattva, relying on the Perfection of Wisdom, finds no obstacle in their mind. **Because there are no obstacles, they have no fear.** Leaving all distorted dream-thinking far behind, they attain Ultimate Nirvana."

"All Buddhas of the past, present, and future, by relying on the Perfection of Wisdom, attain *Anuttara-Samyak-Sambodhi* (Unsurpassed, Complete, and Perfect Enlightenment)."

"Therefore, know that the Perfection of Wisdom is the great transcendent mantra, the great bright mantra, the supreme mantra, the unequaled mantra, which is capable of removing all suffering. This is true, not false."

"Hence, he spoke the Perfection of Wisdom mantra, proclaiming:

Gate gate pāragate pārasaṃgate bodhi svāhā! (Gone, gone, gone beyond, gone altogether beyond, O awakening, hail!)"

"And the light shineth in darkness, and the darkness did not comprehend it."
John 1:5 (Douay–Rheims)

CHAPTER SIXTEEN

Juan Meets Quan(yin): The Moment of Recognition

For fifteen years I had been practicing Zen before I ever read *The Dark Night of the Soul* with any seriousness. I had chanted the *Heart Sutra* hundreds of times. I had sat through grueling, long retreats, wrestled deeply with koans, watched the self dissolve and reassemble, and learned to trust the absolute silence that comes when the mind finally stops trying to hold the world together. I thought I understood emptiness. I thought I thoroughly understood unknowing.

And then I met Juan de la Cruz.

I remember the moment vividly. I was reading his poem slowly, letting each line settle into my chest, when I reached the refrain that runs like a sharp thread through John's entire mystical vision:

Nada, nada, nada. Nothing, nothing, nothing.

The words struck me with a force I did not expect. They didn't feel foreign, and they didn't feel exclusively Christian. They felt like a profound echo — a familiar bell suddenly rung in a completely different monastery.

Because as soon as I heard *"nada,"* I heard something else rising up effortlessly from the deepest wells of my Zen training:

"No eye, no ear, no tongue..."

The two voices — the sixteenth-century Carmelite mystic and the ancient Mahayana sutra — began to harmonize perfectly inside me. John's systematic stripping away of every image of God, every concept, and every spiritual consolation sounded exactly like Avalokiteshvara stripping away the skandhas, the senses, the realms, and the very scaffolding of the separate self.

I watched the maps align point for point:

— John said: *"To reach the All, desire to reach nothing."*

— The Sutra said: *"No attainment, and nothing to attain."*

— John said: *"The soul must empty itself of all that is not God."*

— The Sutra said: *"Form is emptiness, emptiness is form."*

They were not contradicting each other in the slightest. They were completing each other.

In that single moment, something in me clicked into place — not as a clever philosophical idea, but as absolute recognition. It was a deep, bodily knowing. A visceral sense that I had been walking two paths that were, in truth, one single path all along.

The apophatic ascent of John — the journey into the God beyond all human images — was the exact same journey as the *Heart Sutra*'s descent into emptiness. The Christian "dark night" and the Buddhist "emptiness" were not two different experiences. They were simply two different languages describing the same luminous absence, the same spacious presence, and the same radical letting go.

It was as if Juan and Quan Yin, the Chinese incarnation of Avalokiteshvara, had been calling out to each other across centuries, across cultures, and across the terrain of my own divided heart. And I had finally lived enough, practiced enough, suffered enough, and surrendered enough to hear them speaking in perfect unison.

In that moment, the Mountain finally revealed itself.

Not two peaks.

Not two paths.

Not two truths

One summit.

One silence.

One luminous dark.

73

“For behold the kingdom of God is within you.”
Luke 17:21 (Douay–Rheims)

CHAPTER SEVENTEEN

Two Become One

By the time I had lived with *The Dark Night of the Soul* and the *Heart Sutra* long enough for them to truly seep into the marrow of my daily practice, something entirely unexpected began to happen. These were not texts I studied the way one standardly studies academic scripture. They were practical manuals — dynamic guides for letting go, for radical unknowing, and for walking straight into the luminous dark. I practiced them far more than I read them. I breathed them far more than I ever analyzed them.

Over time, the two distinct voices — Juan's relentless *"nada, nada, nada"* and Avalokiteshvara's sweeping *"no eye, no ear, no tongue"* — began to naturally echo each other inside my chest. They arose not as clever philosophical ideas, but as visceral movements of the heart. One systematically stripped away mental images of God; the other stripped away rigid images of the self. One completely emptied the soul; the other completely emptied the *skandhas*. One called the resulting darkness God's merciful hiddenness; the other called it emptiness. Yet both were pointing toward the exact same ungraspable Truth.

Eventually, the artificial boundary between them dissolved entirely. I could no longer tell where the Spanish Carmelite ended and the Eastern Bodhisattva began. Their core teachings braided themselves together in my daily practice, in my breath, and in the exact way I understood the Mountain I had been laboriously climbing for decades.

And then, one day, a poem arrived.

It did not feel like something I had intellectually composed. It felt like an expression that had been slowly forming for years — in *zazen*, in contemplative prayer, in absolute silence, in trauma-suffering, and in final surrender — that had finally found its voice.

What follows is not a clinical interpretation of either ancient text. It is the exact, sacred location where they met inside my own skin. It is the threshold where Juan meets Quan Yin. It is the Dark Night walking directly into Emptiness and discovering that they are the exact same doorway.

<u>Into the Dark Night of Emptiness:
Juan meets Quan(yin)</u>

To arrive at what you do not know,
walk the path that unravels knowing.
To hold what you do not own,
let even the breath in your throat fall away.

Nada, nada, nada.

The sky collapses into the mirror,
the mirror shatters into light.
Form is emptiness, emptiness is form—
a landscape unwritten,
a silence that sees without eyes.

No ears to net the wind,
no tongue to divide bitter from sweet,
no mind to spin its web of thought.
The soul becomes a room stripped bare,
a chamber where God hides by becoming everything.

Nada, nada, nada.

Old age and death dissolve like mist;
suffering leaves no footprint on the stone.
The body loosens its hold on the earth,
the self a candle blown out in the sun.

There is no path, no mountain, no prize—
only the luminous dark,
perfectly empty,
perfectly awake.

“. . .as I have loved you, love one another.”
John 13:34 (Douay–Rheims)

EPILOGUE

The Mountain and the Mirror

There is a moment on every true pilgrimage when the path stops being a path and becomes a mirror. You look up expecting to see the final summit, and instead you see yourself — not the separate self you have laboriously carried for years, but the one that has been quietly forming beneath every step, every breath, and every radical letting go.

When I first began this journey, I thought I was making a definitive choice between conflicting traditions. I thought Zen and Catholicism were two entirely different worlds, two different languages, and two incompatible ways of naming the Real. I believed, with a sense of anxiety, that I had to decide which one was truly mine.

But the Mountain had other plans.

Zen taught me how to empty the mind; Catholicism taught me how to open the heart. Together, they taught me how to see.

The Dark Night stripped me of every rigid image of God.

The *Heart Sutra* stripped me of every defensive image of self.

Together, they revealed a boundless silence that was neither exclusively Buddhist nor Christian, but simply and utterly true.

Along the way, the necessary teachers appeared at their designated thresholds — Aquinas with his luminous simplicity, John with his dark night, RAMBAM with his apophatic silence, Thầy with his gentle compassion, Seung Sahn with his sudden thunder, Chinul with his gradual clarity, de Caussade with his sacrament of the present moment, and Merton with his universal bridge. They did not lead me to different places. They reliably led me to the exact same threshold.

And when I finally possessed the courage to step through, I discovered that the One I had been seeking was not waiting for me at the summit at all.

He had been walking with me the entire time.

The Mountain is God. The Mirror is God. The silence that vibrates between them is God.

Zen has not replaced my Catholicism.

Catholicism has not replaced my Zen.

They have beautifully braided themselves together into a single, cohesive way of seeing — a single way of listening, and a single way of being fully present to the world.

If this book has a definitive purpose, it is not to intellectualize, to persuade, or to compare. It is simply to testify:

There are many paths up the Mountain.

There is only one summit.

And the silence at the top speaks every language.

I do not know where your individual path will lead you. I only know this:

Walk with absolute sincerity.

Walk with active compassion.

Walk with an open hand.

Walk with an uncluttered heart.

And when the Mountain finally reveals itself to your eyes, may you recognize, with a sudden shock of joy, the One who has been walking beside you from the very beginning.

AUTHOR'S NOTE

No one walks the Mountain alone.

Although this book is the singular story of my own journey, it has unfolded entirely within a beautiful community of companions whose steady presence has anchored my steps and brightened my path.

I want to offer a deep, special word of gratitude to Father Peter Nam Tran, OAD, whose genuine friendship and dedicated pastoral care have accompanied me through the vulnerabilities of my journey "back home" into Catholicism. He is a bright young priest with a missionary's heart, and his consistent encouragement has been a quiet, unexpected grace in my life.

I am equally grateful for the many guides, teachers, and friends who have walked beside me across both great traditions. As both Buddhism and Christianity beautifully teach, spiritual friends are not merely a helpful addition — they are the whole of the holy life. Their combined wisdom, patience, and active compassion have shaped the marrow of my bones far more than any book or static doctrine ever could.

To all who have shared this path with me — in deep silence, in prayer, in late-night conversation, or simply in quiet presence — thank you. This book is, in many ways, a direct reflection of the light you have carried.

ONE DHARMA ZEN
Mindfulness - Compassion - Wisdom